the card book

the card book

SUSAN ATTENBOROUGH

PHOTOGRAPHY BY ANNA HODGSON

A Dorling Kindersley book

LONDON, NEW YORK, SYDNEY, DELHI,
PARIS, MUNICH, and JOHANNESBURG

Senior Editor **Heather Jones**
Senior Art Editor **Wendy Bartlet**
Designer **Louise Pudwell**
Category Publisher **Judith More**
Art Director **Janis Utton**
Production Manager **Sarah Coltman**
DTP Designer **Sonia Charbonnier**

First published in Great Britain in 2001 by
Dorling Kindersley Limited
80 Strand, London WC2R ORL

Copyright © 2001
Dorling Kindersley Limited

A CIP catalogue record for this book is available
from the British Library.

ISBN 0-7513-3369-7

Reproduced by Colourscan Overseas Co. Pte. Ltd.,
Singapore
Printed and bound by
Star Standard Industries Pty, Singapore

see our complete catalogue at
www.dk.com

contents

introduction

Making your own cards is fun. It is also a very personal way to greet your friends. Somehow, once you have begun the tradition, it is very hard to buy a card: however beautifully made, no commercial purchase carries the individuality of your own work.

This book features 30 cards based around 12 different techniques, with several variations. Many of the crafts used could become a hobby in themselves and you can find whole books to tell you more about them.

Using specialist tools for some of the techniques will be easier or more effective, but you may not wish to make the investment for a few cards. Some basic equipment is essential for many of the designs. You may prefer to use scissors or a craft knife: it's often a matter of personal preference, but sometimes only one or the other will do. Whether knife or scissors, keep blades sharp, and use and store safely.

These designs rely heavily upon skilled choice of material. Colour is a matter of taste, while texture and thickness will also affect the way your card cuts or folds, as well as the final look. Papers always seem thinner in a large sheet. Making in bulk takes time and needs to be carefully planned. When using a template for a run of cards, do not use your original. As the photocopy becomes degraded, you can make a new copy from the original.

Most important of all, treat the designs here as a springboard for your own originality. Pick and choose. Adapt ideas and colourways. Modify cards for different occasions. Explore and have fun.

christmas

Christmas is a great time to send a hand-made card to someone special – or to get a production line going and make lots for all your friends and family! You can be as contemporary as you like by reworking the traditional themes in new and unusual ways. Many of the world's religions share common symbols and images. The Festivals section may also give you ideas for Christmas cards.

hologram bauble

This glitzy hanging card celebrates the sparkle of Christmas in style, and can look especially dramatic if set where light can catch it and make the colours in the hologrammed plastic flare into life. Such greetings double as decorations and will find a place on the tree, under a mantle, or even on a convenient hook. A hand-delivered card could even incorporate a tiny bauble or bell at its centre.

Follow the instructions on pages 92–93, using the templates on page 107. Add a greeting by writing directly on the outermost ring of the bauble — a fine overhead transparency pen will work on a plasticized surface — or hang a further paper shape from the lowest point of your card for your message.

holly and berry

A familiar Christmas motif is given a cool, contemporary twist using stylized leaf forms and translucent, lime-green paper. When the card is opened, the spiky holly leaves spin independently on the same axis within a frame of ice-white card.

Use the templates on page 104 and the slot-in instructions on pages 88–89. The foil circles that form the centre berry are small and light so the thread must be fine and flexible if the finished berry is to hang properly. You can use the holly leaves to make free-hanging decorations for the Christmas tree or mantelpiece too. Simply omit the slots, and taper the top of template B. Punch a hole at one end for a fine ribbon or thread loop.

golden bell

A traditional motif, crafted from metal foil, is trimmed with an array of very fine, satiny ribbons that act as a softening contrast and enable the recipient to hang your greeting on their tree.

Adapt the instructions for embossing on pages 80–81, using one of the templates on page 106. Thread a toning bead on gold thread and tape unobtrusively to the back, so that it looks like a clapper.

You can send the bell just as it is, or mount it on a card for presentation – make a cut at the centre top of the front of a piece of folded card and push the loop of ribbon in. Alternatively, the bell can be treated as the Silver Fish on pages 31–35, mounted on some luxury silk or fine velvet in rich jewel-like colours for a truly opulent effect.

twirling tree

A simple shape is turned into a sophisticated card mobile in dark green craft foam strips linked by silver-lined glass beads. The heavy base bead ensures that the tree hangs well so that the overall triangle shape appears and disappears as the foam strips swing in and out of alignment.

Follow the cutting foam technique on pages 86–87 using the template on page 107. Write your greeting on a paper strip that matches the foam and then stick it onto the lowest strip of foam with a dry glue roller or double-sided tape.

For a wintry effect, use white foam and dribble white glitter glue along the top of each piece, letting it occasionally trickle down the sides. Leave the glue to dry thoroughly before assembling the tree.

snow crystal

Slow and fiddly rather than difficult, this simple, tranquil design reflects the six-pointed symmetry of an individual snow crystal, and is built up with assorted quilled paper rolls on a paper framework.

Follow the instructions on pages 98–99 and the underlay guide on page 106. Use cool colours, lifting the white with touches of pastel blue, mauve, or silver-grey. To hang the crystal, thread decorative thread through the tip of one arm as shown on page 99. Hang a matching paper hexagon from the lowest arm in the same way for the greeting.

To make the design freestanding, glue the crystal onto card, as in the Rustic Sunflower on pages 68–69. The central star of the original design makes an effective gift tag glued onto a pale blue frosted card.

evergreen ring

An arrangement of tiny Christmas evergreen leaves and silvery sparkles looks suitably festive on a satin-gold card. The ring of pearly cream three-dimensional fabric paint dots is reminiscent of the mistletoe's berries.

The layering technique on pages 82–83 is simplified here to frame tiny holly and mistletoe sprigs, using the templates on page 106. Choose a thin, crisp paper as it is easiest to cut – a high-laid type of paper will give a subtle self pattern.

Change the feel of the card by using other Christmas evergreens. A glossy green holly leaf with shiny red berries, perhaps entwined by ivy leaves, would lend a more traditional air. The card works well too as a tiny gift tag, or even as a motif applied to a plain gift wrapping.

dancing snowmen

This jolly bunch are all individuals. Each is slightly different in shape, size, or detail and all carry traditional Christmas candy canes to complement their dapper top-hat-and-tails image.

Use the templates on page 116 and follow the stand-up technique on pages 100–101. To make the canes, twist together a silver and a red-coated 5mm (⅕in) copper wire and bend the twisted wire around a fine pencil, thick kebab stick, or equivalent to ensure an even curve to the hook. Hats and ties are fixed in place with double-sided tape.

Tiny silver stars form the only other ornamentation and the overall impact of the card relies upon this understatement and the textured white paper used both for the stand-up itself and the outer card.

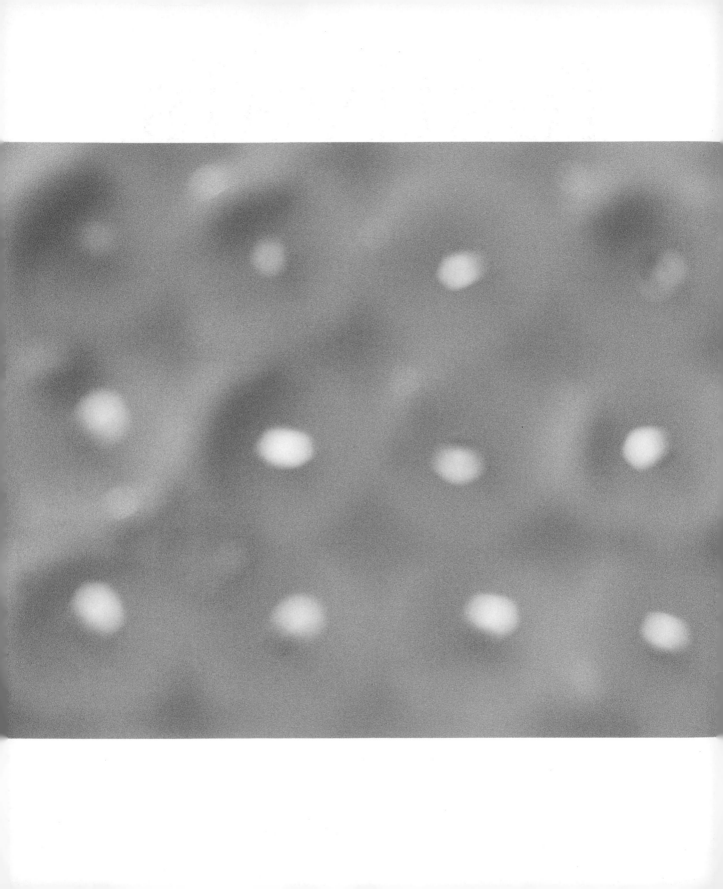

festivals

Festivals of different faiths are celebrated all around us, in today's multicultural society. There are cards here that have been inspired by symbols and events from the Islamic, Hindu, Jewish, and Christian calendars. Some eternal symbols even seem to cross from faith to faith. Make and send a card for your own special occasion, or to acknowledge and share a friend's celebration.

candle glow

Light, especially from a candle, is one of the world's most enduring spiritual symbols. A candle carries a message of hope, of triumph over adversity, or simply of peace. This card would be appropriate to celebrate the festivals of Diwali, Hanukkah or Christmas.

It is made using the simple pop-up technique on pages 84–85 and the template on page 113. Use three papers with different textures: this example employs a matt lavender paper, a shiny purple metallic paper, and a lustrous pearly cream card. The colours of the flame repeat the colours of the card, but you may prefer more realistic hues. Substitute matte and shiny gold for the two outer papers and this card becomes a handsome way to mark a golden wedding anniversary.

star of david

This design is perfect for a card to greet the Jewish New Year, as well as other festivals within that calendar. The star's shape lends itself well to the repeating concertina design, and forms a pleasing composition when the card is closed too. When it is opened up, the golden stars reflect in each other if the paper is shiny enough.

Follow the concertina technique on pages 90–91 and use the open star templates on page 108.

Make a special envelope for this one (see pages 122–123), adding a simple border with gold ink as a finishing touch. The star is a versatile motif and you could even modify these open stars, to send wishes for success in examinations.

moon and stars

Particularly associated with the Muslim Eid festivals, both Eid al-Fitr and Eid al-Adha, a crescent moon and stars can be used in celebration of many events, in many faiths. Midnight-blue rings contrast with the gold, and create striking shadows if appropriately hung.

Follow the spheres technique on pages 96–97 and the templates on page 109. For the stars, cut-outs are highly effective, but be careful not to weaken the card by cutting too close to the edge of the rings. Use gummed merit stars in between, trimmed to size.

Vary the design by using silver motifs or using only one style of star. The crescent moon could be replaced by a larger central star to create a Christmas mood, with perhaps a neutral or satin metallic paper.

easter egg

A deliciously eggy-yellow two-tone material gives extra interest to this sleek and elegant design for a golden easter egg, both when the card is folded flat as it emerges from the envelope and when it is open, while fine dressmakers' glitter adds a sophisticated sparkle.

The turnstiles technique on pages 94–95 works well with the simple egg shape template on page 110. You can make two-tone card by gluing two pieces of paper evenly all over to stick together back to back if the ready-made sort is unavailable.

Once the card is cut, use a cocktail stick or fine brush to add the finest line of PVA glue all around the cut thickness of each outward-facing arm in turn, then dip in fine glitter powder.

silver fish

The traditional Christian image of a fish is used to create a multi-layered card suitable for many occasions as well as Easter itself; the fish is also associated with good fortune and the astrological sign of Pisces.

Adapt the foil embossing technique on pages 80–81 and use the fish template on page 110. Mark rows of tiny scales from alternate sides of the foil, then add fin pleats. Dab the foil with thixotropic gel colours, which allow the metallic glint to shine through. Once dry, use double-sided tape to mount the fish onto two different watery papers, then fix to a translucent turquoise plastic. You could use twisted silver wire to replace the foil fish and fix in place by loops of thin wire pushed through the corrugated card before mounting and finish with a silver bead eye.

good luck

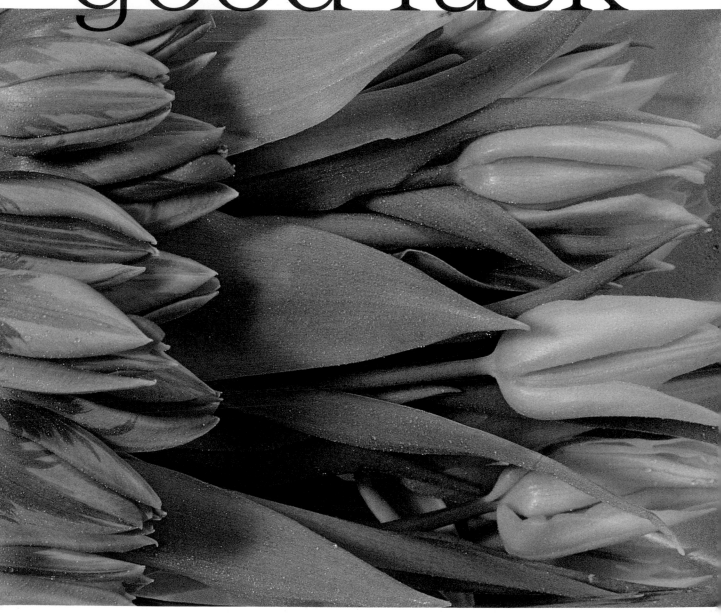

The care that you put into a hand-made card to wish a friend or relation good luck is especially appreciated before a challenging event. Some ideas here are for a specific occasion, others are more general. You could also adapt ideas from other sections; the stand-ups on pages 100–101 or pop-out boxes on pages 102–103 could feature appropriate motifs for the coming event.

farewell wishes

This is a useful design for a departing friend or colleague. An old-fashioned fountain pen pops up and a glossy trail of apparently wet ink flows freely onto a piece of high-quality writing paper.

Follow the stand-ups technique on pages 100–101, and the templates on page 111. Black craft foam gives the pen real thickness, but stiff paper would work too. The golden mirriboard used for the traditional nib is also repeated in the double-sided framing layer, and relief fabric paint represents the ink. The paint is slow to dry right through, so allow plenty of time before closing the card.

You could replace the abstract line with a farewell message or use a modern pen shape and colours to bring the card more up-to-date.

lucky horseshoe

This coolly sophisticated good-luck card takes its anthracite theme from the horseshoe which is cut from a dark-grey pearly metallic paper, decorated with a silver pen, glued firmly upright, and complemented by sparkly, silvery shapes.

Follow the instructions on pages 82–83 and use the simple template on page 111. Several flat toning paper shapes, rhinestones, sequins, and stick-ons are used to complete the mini-composition behind the acetate.

To jazz things up, add further glitz with a metallic or shiny black card to complement the silver theme, or use quite different, jewel-bright colourways. You can adapt this design to suit specific events: tiny "L" plates for a driving test or packing cases for a house move, for example.

four-leaf clover

This attractive card is a variation on the basic pop-up, although the more complex lines give it a quite different feel from the simple pop-up on pages 26–27, and it requires no further decoration.

Adapt the simple pop-up technique on page 84–85, with the template on page 115. A high-gloss green mirriboard mount sparkles against the subtly textured Ingres paper used for the clover cut-out. You may like to back the mirriboard with the same paper as you used for the clover cut-out to give a satisfying outer finish to the card.

Cut away the tiny decorative windows on each lobe of the clover as shown. Cut the stalk shape away too, and when fixing the two layers together, make sure that the edges of the stalk slit are stuck down.

new home

Designed as a welcome to a new home, this card can be personalized by replacing the heart with a house number, name, or other motif.

The design is a variation on the pendants technique on pages 92–93, with the outer shape cut into the front of a free-standing card. You will find all the templates on page 112. Two sheets of hand-made copper-coloured paper are glued back to back and the heart is cut from a rough ivory paper and hung on plain cotton thread. Infinite variations suggest themselves: you could modify shape, colour, and paper texture to relate more closely to the new home or add a door house number or house name, written on a piece of acetate sandwiched between the two sides of the smallest shape.

romance

A range of romantic events are celebrated here, from the first tentative anonymous Valentine, through courtship, engagement, wedding, and anniversary to ideas for silver and golden wedding celebrations. Unusual materials in traditional and more surprising colours provide several different ways to express your message, from subtle and sophisticated to downright wacky.

rock-solid heart

A monochrome greeting that reflects the idea of a love built to last, this card uses crisp, lightly veined elephant-hide papers in two shades of grey.

Follow the simple pop-up technique on pages 84–85, using the template on page 105. Form the copper wire arrow carefully following the template guide; conceal the ends in the twisted shaft. Ease the arrow through the marked slits, and close the card experimentally to check that it does not catch on the paper.

Brighter colours would work well too. Gold, silver, and colour-coated copper wires are all available to team with papers of your choice. For a more emphatic arrow, wrap tiny scraps of embossing foil smoothly around the head and flight.

soft hearted

The subtle, ivory-cream heart will appeal to the sophisticated romantic

so this could be a suitable card for a Valentine or a wedding anniversary.

To make the heart, adapt the cutting-foam technique on pages 86–87,

using the template on page 118. Here, the foam strips are interspersed

with pairs of silvery seed beads and two flat-backed rhinestones are

glued securely together to create the larger base bead. The window in

the simple, square presentation mount measures 15 x 15cm (6 x 6in)

and the neatly taped loop can easily be detached to hang more

permanently elsewhere. You could choose a colourway to celebrate a

special wedding anniversary – silver, ruby or gold, for example – or

maybe to alternate the favourite colours of both partners.

sweet heart

The thick, slightly frosted, jellybean plastic used for this Valentine is teamed with an embossed silver foil here and hung on transparent nylon thread for a thoroughly modern effect.

Follow the instructions on pages 80–81 and the templates on page 105. It is not easy to cut neat curves on this plastic but you can quickly smooth out any imperfections with fine-gauge sandpaper.

For a contemporary card with an industrial look, substitute a medium-weight metal embossing foil for the plastic mount; take care to avoid sharp edges. For a more traditional approach, hang a golden brass foil heart on silken thread or fine ribbon within a richly coloured paper or fabric-covered mount.

champagne celebration

A card for almost any important celebration, this design looks attractive

as it emerges from its envelope as well as in its opened form.

Adapt the concertina technique on pages 90–91. Use the templates

on pages 120–121, cutting first the glass shapes and then the champagne

itself. Extend the back flap by 1.5cm (½in) an add an extra 10cm (4in)

for the extra motif. The plastic for the glasses needs to have sufficient

body to stand up straight, without being too thick to cut neatly. A frosted

champagne-coloured paper is ideal for pricking with different-sized

needles to create a subtle bubble effect or you could simplify by using

a stiff champagne-coloured card for the glass shapes, merely suggesting

the liquid within by a fine golden outline.

love birds

These amorous love birds make a card suitable for an engagement or wedding. The pearly rings encompassing them add a subtle sparkle, in contrast to the voluptuous pink heart they carry.

Adapt the spheres technique on pages 96–97 and use the templates on pages 108–109. Sandwich the love birds with a hanging thread centrally between two hearts. Push each wing piece carefully through the slot in the birds body to the central fold. Check that everything is balanced and hangs straight.

You could enlarge the birds and fix to a small piece of card to make a gift tag or freestanding greeting. Trim away part of the back wing on each bird and use foam pads to fix the motif slightly proud.

wedding bell

To celebrate a wedding, this silver bell looks good as it emerges from its envelope and transforms into a 3D card when opened and set down.

Follow the turnstiles technique on pages 94–95, and use the templates on pages 114–115. Careful and accurate cutting is vital to ensure the hinge points are both strong and flexible. Two textured papers act as foils to the elegant silver glitter spray – quite different from the traditional sprinkle glitters. The couple's initials could be monogrammed in a corner of the card.

The bell motif is also a traditional Christmas theme: white and gold papers would be attractive, while the more traditional might go for a stronger pairing of colours, such as gold on red.

birthdays

This birthday selection ranges from the surprise of a customized pop-up polyhedron to the gentle evocation of a favourite flower or a mobile for the newest baby. Several reflect a recipient's interests – football, gardening, sailing, shopping even – and may prompt you to experiment. Most could also be used to wish someone better, to send thanks or simply as a general greeting.

camellia bloom

A crisp double camellia with its golden centre was the inspiration for this birthday card. Arrange the individual layers of petals within the card for presentation carefully: it will look more balanced and attractive some ways than others.

Adapt the slot-in technique on pages 88–89, using the templates on page 119. Line a piece of green paper with a deep yellow which will show between the rings of dusky madder paper. You can leave the centre of the flower empty as here or you can emphasize the circle of stamens further by sandwiching a layer of clear acetate between the two layers of paper forming the inner petal shape, and squeezing a ring of dots and stripes onto it in shades of pearly yellow three-dimensional fabric paint.

blue marina

A cheerful, summery card for sailors and water-lovers, using pale blue textured paper for the sea and sky, with tiny blue hulls and individually patterned pennants to co-ordinate.

Follow the stand-up technique on pages 100–101 and templates on page 116. High-laid white paper for the boats suggests sails, with further detail added in ink or paper collage. You could add a simple circle of gold or silver paper to the background for the sun or moon. An impossibly blue sea is evoked by the paper used for the envelope but you will need to add a contrast address panel if the card is to be posted.

This is an infinitely variable technique: from dogs or cats, to flowers or vintage cars – select a motif appropriate to any event.

birthday surprise

You need a relatively stout, snug-fitting envelope for this birthday surprise; powered by its elastic band, the card should literally spring out of its covering to greet the recipient.

Full instructions for the technique appear on pages 102–103, and the template is on page 117. Absolute accuracy in marking, cutting and matching the two pieces is vital for a sleek and impressive shape.

You can personalize the polyhedron in any number of ways before assembly. Glue tiny paper cut-outs, use miniature stencils or rubber stamps or experiment with black-on-white op art effects to decorate each facet of the polyhedron. Plan the design carefully to achieve a balanced effect when the shape springs open.

rustic sunflower

The earthy tones and slightly rough papers of this sunflower card will appeal to many a no-nonsense gardener. It might also be appropriate for a child with a pack of seeds tucked inside to spark a new interest.

This card is based on the technique on pages 98–99. Use the template on page 118 as a guide, working from the tight coils of the flower's centre. Four strips begin the stem; the innermost two joined right to the flower, while the outermost curl away to form the leaf stems.

When the flower is complete, brush its underside with PVA glue, position on the folded card mount, and fix leaves in places. Add a margin line in gold. Try quilling small flowers with thinner papers in soft pastels for a more traditional look.

spinning teddy

A card that can be sent in celebration of a new arrival as well as to celebrate an early birthday, it could be hung as a mobile above a baby's cot or changing mat.

Adapt the spheres technique on pages 96–97, using the teddy template on page 108 and the moon and stars template on page 109. A crisp, mottled paper in a soft lilac encircles a central teddy cut from a cloudy white paper. Add pearly lilac metallic paws and features using a gel pen, and hang the teddy from a silky lilac thread.

As an alternative to the classic pastels, try bolder, bright, contrasting colours for a more contemporary approach, or choose colours to complement the baby's sleeping area.

slotted cogs

Precision cutting and modern, hand-finished papers produce a strong greeting for the mechanically minded. Arrange the cogs with care when you close the card: they will swing into their own positions when open.

Adapt the slot-in technique on pages 88–89 using the templates on page 120. Note the tilted axis: the cogs are set diagonally. For the cogs, back a rough, holey silver-grey paper with shiny silver paper. Cut in two and glue back to back. Line a contrasting pale golden-grey paper with black for the window card mount.

The card's rugged feel could be given a different slant by the substitution of fine high-gloss and filigree-gold papers to suggest precision antique watch or clock mechanisms.

expanding football

For football fanatics – make sure that you choose the right team colours

for the tassel and hanging loop.

Follow the technique on pages 102–103, using the template on page

117 and white card that will not buckle once inked or painted. Paint

alternate rhomboids and one of the hexagonal faces black after scoring:

it helps contain the colour. Mark the central point on both hexagons and

pierce to attach the loop and tassel before assembly. For the loop, twist

together ribbon, lampshade yarn, or embroidery silks. For the tassel, wrap

the yarns around two fingers, slip off, and secure around one end before

cutting the loops at the other. Push a strand of yarn through the loop of

tassel and the hole to fasten inside before assembling the polyhedron.

birthday boxes

This array of birthday parcels shows off a carefully gathered collection of papers, linked by a common colour theme.

Adapt the concertina technique on pages 90–91 for four motifs, cutting the card 10cm (4in) longer and use the templates on page 121. Plain and small patterned papers work best for this card, all set on a neutral background concertina. Matching ribbons of different widths link the parcel. Wrap ribbons around to the back at top and and bottom and stick with fabric glue and finish with matching bows.

The use of different papers instantly alters the mood, from dainty or subtle to bright and bold. A matching envelope made from one of the patterned papers makes the card particularly special.

techniques

& templates

Here you will find step-by-step instructions to the basic techniques and all the templates you need to help you make your own cards. Specific variations for individual designs are explained in the project section. If templates require frequent handling, photocopy directly onto thin card if your machine allows this, or glue a paper photocopy onto card before cutting out.

Sweet Heart
See page 52

embossing

This technique uses shallow surface impressions, worked from both sides of the material, to create relief decoration on lightweight metal foil.

Photocopy both templates on page 105 onto thin card and cut out, following the outer line of template A. Use scissors to cut a small piece of foil and transfer template A to the foil by drawing round the outline with the pencil. Try to avoid touching the foil whenever possible because it is easily fingermarked.

Cut round the marked outline, holding the waste foil wherever possible. In step 3 you will be cutting down template A so if you plan to make several Sweet Hearts, prepare the foil hearts now and carry out each instruction on all cards stage by stage. Alternatively, make several copies of template A.

Reduce template A to the next largest heart size by cutting on the line nearest to the edge. Centre the smaller template A on the foil heart and emboss its outline into the metal by drawing round it. Reduce template A to the next size and repeat. Reduce again and reverse the foil to emboss the remaining lines.

Golden Bell
See page 14

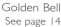

For the Sweet Heart you will need:

Templates on page 105 • Thin card • Lightweight artist's metal foil • Scissors • Hard, sharp pencil or embossing tool • Pink polypropelene or card • Ruler • Craft knife • Cutting mat • Fine sandpaper • Strong needle • Fine nylon thread

Silver Fish
See page 34

Now begin to make a series of contrasting patterns between the embossed lines. Here the outermost zone is given a pleated effect. First mark a series of even, well-spaced radial lines, using the pencil; then turn the heart over and bissect each of the spaces between the lines with another embossed line.

Work inwards through the zones, alternating plain and patterned bands. To make a zigzag pattern, mark the basic shape from edge to edge of the band and then turn the metal and add unconnected 'v's within the spaces in the pattern. Finally, press a series of dots from both sides into the inner lobes.

Cut a mount 20cm × 15cm (7⅞ × 5⅚in) with the craft knife. Score to fold. Using template B, mark the heart, cut out, and sand to finish. Bore a hole in the plastic just above the cutout, and at the top of the foil. Thread a nylon loop through the plastic, and pull the ends through. Thread the foil onto one end and tie.

Lucky Horseshoe
See page 40

layering

Contrasting but complementary papers are arranged to create a subtly textured frame which adds depth to a simple, small-scale composition.

Fold the blue base paper in half, scoring with a craft knife if necessary; then cut to make a card 13 × 13cm (5¹/8 × 5¹/8in) square. Cut a 10 × 10cm (4in × 4in) square of grey paper and an acetate square 9.5 × 9.5cm (3³/4 × 3³/4in). Glue the grey square centrally on the card front, setting the acetate aside for step 5.

Cut the innermost, white square, measuring 6 × 6cm (2³/8x 2³/8in), from fine corrugated paper. The effect will be more interesting if you cut so that the ribs run diagonally across the square, but take care to ensure that they are not squashed or snagged in the process. Glue the shape centrally on the grey square.

Use the template on page 111 to cut a horseshoe from metallic paper. Begin to explore different compositions using the horseshoe as the focus of your design and trying out sequins, flat rhinestones and silver-paper or hologrammed stars. Take care not to overcrowd the arrangement.

For the Lucky Horseshoe you will need:

Two toning papers • Craft knife • Cutting mat • Ruler • Pencil • Scissors • Acetate sheet • Glue stick • Fine corrugated paper • Template on page 111 • Metallic paper • Toning sequins, rhinestones and stick-ons • All-purpose glue • Three-dimensional metallic craft or fabric paint

Evergreen Ring
See page 20

Decorate the horseshoe with a silver metallic pen to represent nail holes before glueing in its final position. Then stick or glue most of the remaining elements in place. A cocktail stick or pin is helpful when applying glue to tiny pieces. Set aside a few extra sequins to shuffle freely behind the acetate.

Squeeze dots of all-purpose glue all round the grey border that surrounds the white square, placing them at about 12cm (1/2in) intervals from the outer edge of the paper. These will secure the acetate. Add the loose sequins, position the acetate and weight the glue lines from the outside until dry.

Using a complementary metallic-effect paint, pipe neat, peaked dots round the acetate, both to conceal the glue spots and to add a final decorative touch. It's worth practising on spare acetate first. Allow plenty of time for the paint to dry: it shrinks slightly and the peaks will squash if pressed too soon.

Candle Glow
See page 26

pop-ups

A single sheet of paper is cut, folded and mounted on backing card to achieve the element of surprise in this three-dimensional effect.

Photocopy the templates on page 113. Cut a piece of cream card to the same size as the square template and secure the template to the right side of the card with strips of removable tape. Using the craft knife and straight edge, cut through both layers just along the solid lines of the candle shape.

Use the craft knife (or scoring tool) and straight edge as a guide to score only the dotted lines on the template. Carefully remove the template from the card, detaching the tape. Gently ease the spine above and below the candle shape downwards into a 'valley' fold and the candle itself upwards into a 'mountain'

Cut two squares for the mount: the inner, shiny one 17 × 17cm (6⅝ × 6⅝in) and the matt one approx. 18 × 18cm (7 ⅛ × 7 ⅛in). Fold each square in half, scoring if necessary. Glue the purple papers together at the spines and then the edges. Finally attach the pop-up, glueing only the valley folds and outer edges.

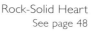

Four-Leaf Clover
See page 42

Rock-Solid Heart
See page 48

For the Candle Glow you will need:

Templates on page 113 • Glossy cream card • Pencil • Ruler • Craft knife • Cutting mat • Removable tape • Scoring tool (optional) • Straight edge • Scissors • Metallic paper • Toning double-faced matt paper • All-purpose glue • Toning metallic paper scraps in three colours

Plan the colour sequence of the metallic paper scraps and use the flame templates to draw and cut out the three shapes. Small-bladed or manicure scissors may help. Paper-backed metallics are often easier to mark on the reverse, but be sure to turn the templates so the shapes still echo the curve of the flame.

Assemble the three-layered metallic flame, arranging the smaller shapes so that they lie almost at the wide base of the largest shape. Use just the tiniest dots of glue and leave to dry thoroughly. A cocktail stick or the head of a pin is a useful way to control the amount of glue you apply.

Open the card to check the position of the flame decoration: it should lie very near the base of the cream flame shape. Lay the opened card flat and glue the decoration to the pop-up. You could, as a final touch, cut a second decoration and glue it to the bottom corner of the otherwise plain cover.

Twirling Tree
See page 16

cutting foam

Densely textured yet featherlight, coloured craft foam is cut and assembled to create a perfectly balanced and ever-changing hanging card.

Photocopy the Twirling Tree template on page 106 and rule a faint line between the centre points. Using a pair of fine scissors, cut out from the template each of the strips that make the tree shape (if you prefer, use a craft knife and ruler). Using the template this way will make the best use of your foam.

Place each template strip on top of the foam and draw the outlines of the strips onto the foam using the pencil. Use a ruler or other straight edge to guide you. Cut out the strips of foam. You should finish with seven pieces each measuring approximately 1cm (½in), including the triangle for the top of the tree.

To indicate the line of the hanging thread, lightly but firmly mark the centre point of each section by scratching with the needle across the thickness of the foam at the top and bottom. The centre line ruled through the entire template before the sections were cut out will guide you or use a ruler as shown.

For the Twirling Tree you will need:

Template on page 106 • Ruler • Pencil • Scissors • Craft foam
• Craft knife • Straight edge • Cutting mat • Needle • Fine
metallic thread • Shiny seed beads to complement main bead
• Large, heavy bead • All-purpose glue

Soft Hearted
See page 50

Cut a length of thread more than twice as tall as the tree (allowing for a loop and for finishing off), double it and thread the ends through the eye of the needle. Carefully ease the needle and thread straight down through the foam at the centre points of the triangle, leaving a good loop for hanging.

Thread three seed beads after the triangle. Repeat, threading each section through the thickness of the foam at the exact centre to ensure perfect balance and following with three more beads until all the sections are threaded. Add only two beads after the final section and then the larger bead.

Thread a last seed bead, passing the needle through twice to hold it securely. Then work the needle back through the beads at the base and the lowest section before cutting the thread. A dot of glue in the bore of the last bead adds extra security. Gently ease all the elements down to avoid gaps if necessary.

Holly and Berry
See page 12

slot-ins

Simple paper engineering: decorative interlocking shapes in different colours slot into a window cut-out to create a three-dimensional design.

Photocopy all four templates on page 104 and cut out template A. Cut a piece of white card measuring 20cm × 15cm (7⁷/₈in × 5⁷/₈in) and fold in half, scoring carefully with a craft knife if needed for a crisp spine. Centre template A on the card front, keeping it perfectly vertical, and draw round it with a pencil.

Carefully cut along the pencil line on the front, using scissors or a craft knife, and discard the white leaf shape. If you choose a craft knife, work on a firm, non-slip surface, such as a cutting mat, and open the card first to avoid marking or cutting right through both sides. Erase any remaining pencil marks.

If you wish, you can fold the back of the card so that the holly leaves at the front are viewed more clearly. Mark a line on the plain back section of the card, parallel to the spine and about 5cm (2in) from it. Scoring lightly if necessary, fold along this line, away from the leaf-shaped window.

Camellia Bloom
See page 62

Slotted Cogs
See page 72

For the Holly and Berry you will need:

Templates on page 104 • Scissors • Craft knife • Cutting mat • Ice white card • Ruler • Pencil • Eraser • Straight edge • Translucent green paper • Red paper foil scraps • Fine green cotton thread • Clear, all-purpose glue • Matt or shiny adhesive tape (optional)

Cut out and discard the inner sections of templates B and C. Use the templates to make two holly leaves, cutting the outside lines first. Assemble to check that the small leaf slots into the large one, and the large leaf fits into the opening, while both can move freely. Shave the inside of the appropriate slot if necessary.

Using the foil paper and berry template, cut out two circles. To ensure a perfect match, you can fold the foil in half and cut both layers together. Lightly glue the fine cotton thread to the back of one circle and then cover with the second, aligning them carefully back to back, to create a double-sided red berry.

Remove the leaves from the card and check the position of the berry – it should hang centrally within the hole on the small leaf. Trim the thread to allow a slight overlap onto the leaf and secure unobtrusively: how will depend on the leaf material and may be shiny or matt adhesive tape or clear glue. Re-assemble.

Star of David
See page 28

concertinas

A repeated motif, varied only in size and mounted on folded paper: this design can easily be extended by adding 10cm (4in) for every extra fold.

From creamy paper stiff enough to support the motifs, cut out a rectangle 42 × 12cm (16½ × 4¾in). Measuring from one end, lightly mark both edges of the paper at 12cm (4¾in) and then at 5cm (2in) intervals to indicate fold lines. Score lightly along each line if necessary, using a straight edge to link marks.

Carefully fold the strip along the scored lines, first one way and then the other to make the concertina shape as shown. The long section at one end will act as a backing frame for the motifs when the card is closed. If the scored lines are perfectly accurate, all the layers will overlap exactly at the sides.

Photocopy the star templates on page 108 and cut out. Use glue stick or another quick-drying, non-wrinkling adhesive to back a small sheet of gold paper with more stiff paper. Position the templates on the gold paper with tiny strips of removable tape, taking any grain into account, and mark the star outline.

For the Star of David you will need:

Stiff cream paper or thin card • Ruler • Pencil • Scissors
• Craft knife • Cutting mat • Straight edge • Templates on
page 108 • Glue stick • Glossy gold paper, possibly textured
• Removable tape • Double-sided tape

Champagne Celebration
See page 54

Birthday Boxes
See page 76

Using the craft knife, cut round the pencil outline and then through the template and the papers to release and discard the waste segments. A straight edge can be helpful: place it against each diagonal and horizontal in turn, cutting all the relevant lines along it accurately. Remove the templates carefully.

Centre the largest star on the front of the concertina section nearest the backing frame. The top of the star's lowest horizontal bar aligns with the fold itself and its upper points are framed by the backing flap when the concertina is closed. Secure with a strip of double-sided tape along the fold.

Complete the sequence of three in the same way, working forwards and using the smallest star last. Before securing, check that each of the smaller stars will sit centrally upon the preceding star when the card is closed. Use a craft knife to trim away any cream paper visible through the inner spaces of the stars.

Hologram Bauble
See page 10

pendants

Repeating cut-paper shapes set one within the other for a design inspired by a set of Russian dolls; holographic and metallic papers give added depth.

Photocopy the templates on page 107. Plan the sequence of papers, alternating colour and finish. There are two ways to cut the shapes. Method 1: cut out templates A to D, discarding the centres of A to C; mark and cut two shapes for all four templates from your chosen papers.

Method 2: rough cut templates A to D; fold each paper with right sides together, secure the four templates to your chosen papers, using removable tape, and cut through all the layers at once. Whichever method you use, work on the white reverse of holographic material. Set aside shapes to be glued in steps 4 and 5.

Using template E and foil, cut two shapes to decorate the top of the card. You can, if you prefer, cut both shapes out together. Again, fold a small piece of foil in half, right sides facing, before placing the straight edge of the template to the fold, marking and cutting out; turn right sides out without cutting the fold.

For the Hologram Bauble you will need:

Templates on page 107 • Holographic and metallic papers in four complementary colours • Scissors • Pencil • Removable tape (optional) • Scrap of gold or silver foil • Fine decorative thread • All-purpose glue • Needle (optional)

New Home
See page 44

Cut the doubled thread to reach from the centre of the card up beyond the outer ring, allowing for a generous hanging loop. Glue both ends to the back of one central circle, making sure the threads emerge together from one side. Add more glue and lower the other circle, right side up, into place.

Repeat the process with the other pairs of shapes. Working outwards, keep the threads taut and centre each ring on the previous one. Take great care to ensure perfect alignment at every stage, checking the fit on both sides before the glue dries. Fine papers require drier glues: experiment on scraps if in doubt.

To finish, glue the cap into position, points downwards, just where the looped thread emerges. If you cut two separate shapes, then simply place one on each side. If you cut two from a folded piece of paper, use a needle to thread the loop carefully through the centre of the fold and slide into place before glueing.

Wedding Bell
See page 58

turnstiles

Simple but perfectly accurate paper cutting creates an appealing three-dimensional form that reflects a pedestrian turnstile with horizontal, radiating arms.

Photocopy the template A on page 114 and cut out the frame. Cut a slightly larger square of white paper and centre A on it with removable tape. Use a craft knife and straight edge to cut the horizontal lines through both layers, working from the centre. Cut the solid outline of the bell to release alternate arms.

Photocopy template B on page 115 and cut out. Place in the centre of a square of the translucent paper, allowing a wide margin all round. Cut out and discard the bell shape. Some textured papers are easier to cut with sharp scissors – to avoid dragging – but you will have to draw round the template first.

Check that any pencil lines are fully cut away before you position the translucent paper frame accurately on the white paper. The bell-shaped cut-out should align exactly with the bell outline on the paper. Glue the two together. Choice of glue will depend on the papers used: it must not show through.

For the Wedding Bell you will need:

Templates on pages 114–115 • Scissors • Stiff white paper
• Removable tape • Craft knife • Cutting mat • Straight edge
• Translucent, white handmade paper • All-purpose glue • Scoring
tool (optional) • Waste paper • Newspaper • Silver glitter spray

Easter Egg
See page 32

Turn the card over and trim the translucent paper flush with the white paper. Referring to the dotted lines on A, score the back very accurately against a straight edge along the spine at the tiny vertical hinge points as above and below the bell. Ease the card to fold with the translucent paper outside.

Lay the open card down, face up, to mask for final decoration. Cut a piece of strong waste paper almost in half and slip it under the bell's 'arms' on both sides of the hinges. Ensure that each side of the paper butts as snugly as possible to the centre and tape the slit at the bottom to prevent seepage.

Mask a large area in a well-ventilated room with newspaper and, following manufacturer's instructions, spray a series of fine mists of glitter over the exposed areas, allowing each layer to dry before spraying again. This creates a much more effective finish than one or two thicker coats. When dry, remove the mask.

Moon and Stars
See page 30

spheres

Simple cutting, acccurate scoring and careful folding create a subtle and elegant form that plays on the idea of two pairs of circles at right angles to each other.

Photocopy the templates on page 109. Cut round the outer lines of the semi-circles template and tape to the card. Working with a craft knife, cut the semi-circles on one side and then the other, taking care not to extend the lines. You could cut the semi-circles with a bladed compass, using the centre dot.

Using a straight edge, score down the intermittent dotted lines which separate the semi-circles. Do not extend these hinge points: the unscored sections must be straight and strong. Cut away any waste from around and within the shape, remove the template and ease the card open along the score lines.

Flatten the card again and cut some tiny stars in the semi-circles of paper by superimposing two equal-sided triangles, one point up over one point down. Take care not to weaken the paper by cutting too close to the edge. Check the effect by opening the card again and add stick-on stars, trimmed to fit.

Love Birds
See page 56

Spinning Teddy
See page 70

For the Moon and Stars you will need:

Templates on page 109 • Scissors • Stiff blue paper • Removable tape • Craft knife and (optional) bladed compass • Cutting mat • Straight edge • Stick-on stars • Pencil • Gold or silver paper scraps • Clear, all-purpose glue • Blue cotton • Needle

Cut out both moon templates very neatly and then mark and cut out two crescent moons on a scrap of gold or silver metallic paper. The two crescents will be stuck together, back to back, and suspended by a piece of thread (see step 5). Mark the hanging point discreetly on the top edge of the moons.

Lay one crescent moon face down and, with a dot of glue, secure one end of a short length of cotton so that it extends outwards at the hanging point. Check that the balance is right before adding more glue and lowering the second moon into position. Make sure they are perfectly aligned before leaving them to dry.

To attach the cotton to the top of the inner semi-circle, trim to length and glue. To make the hanger, knot a loop of cotton and, using the needle, thread it through the centre top of the outermost semi-circle; draw the knot through the loop and tighten. Open the card until the semi-circles hang at right angles.

quilling

Narrow cut-paper strips are rolled, shaped and assembled to form delicate lacy designs – this traditional craft is also known as paper filigree.

Snow Crystal
See page 18

Photocopy the underlay on page 106 onto thin card and protect with a sheet of acetate taped into position to avoid slippage. A clear plastic bag will do the job too but take care to secure it firmly. Cut the quilling or lightweight paper into strips 3mm (^{1}/8in) wide, using a sharp craft knife and straight edge.

White and pale blue papers have been prepared here but you may prefer to use white strips throughout. Pre-cut quilling strips are available from craft shops in a wide range of colours but cutting your own from A4 paper does not take long. Be sure to choose a thin, crisp paper.

Glue two white strips together to make a stiff quill of double thickness. When dry, cut a 13.5cm (5^1/4in) length and score the quill six times at 2cm (^{4}/5in) intervals, allowing for a small final overlap. Fold gently at the score marks to form the hexagon, checking for crisp corners. Glue the overlap to secure.

For the Snow Crystal you will need:

Underlay template on page 106 • Thin card • Acetate or clear plastic bag • Adhesive tape • Scissors • Quilling or lightweight paper • Ruler • Craft knife • Cutting mat • Straight edge • PVA glue • Quilling tool or bamboo skewer • Decorative thread

Rustic Sunflower
See page 68

Prepare about 30 tight white rolls from strips 6cm (2¼in) long. The number will depend on the width of the tool you use. Wind each paper up firmly, keeping the roll tight as you secure it with glue, and hold until dry. Place the hexagon on the underlay and, working from the centre outwards, glue the rolls together as shown.

For looser rolls, wind 10cm (4in) long papers but let the roll drop off the tool and unwind to the right diameter before glueing. Make six white 6mm (¼in) diameter rolls, twelve blue and six white 10mm (³⁄₈in) diameter rolls, and six blue 12mm (½in) diameter rolls. Use the underlay and picture to shape rolls as required.

Glue each roll in place, avoiding the underlay as much as you can, although the acetate or plastic will make it possible to detach the snow crystal if necessary. To make the hanger: knot a loop of decorative thread, pass one end through the outermost roll on one arm of the crystal, draw the knotted end through the loop and tighten.

Blue Marina
See page 64

stand-ups

A more elaborate version of the pop-up technique (see pages 82–83): extra motifs are cut and decorated before they are fixed to simple cut-out bars.

Photocopy both templates on page 116, using thin card for the yacht template because you will need to draw round it several times in step 5. Then cut a piece of blue paper to the same size as the pop-up template and secure the template on top of the blue paper, using removable tape.

Cut firmly and neatly through both layers, working along all the solid lines. These form the strips that will become pop-up bars. Use a straight edge for really accurate cutting. Lightly score the dotted lines, taking special care not to extend the scoring along the central fold onto the pop-up bars. Remove the tape.

Ease the paper into a downward, 'valley' fold along the central scored line. This will begin to push the pop-up bars outward – gently fold the scored lines on each bar to make crisp angles. Cut a piece of white card 14.5 × 15.5cm (5³/4 × 6in). Score and fold in half along the shorter side.

Dancing Snowmen
See page 22

Farewell Wishes
See page 38

For Blue Marina you will need:

Templates on page 116 • Thin card • Blue paper • Scissors
• Removable tape • Craft knife • Cutting mat • Straight edge
• White card • Glue stick • Fine scissors • Paper scraps
• Coloured inks or pencils • Double-sided tape (optional)

Apply glue to the spine of the prepared blue pop-up, avoiding the pop-up bars themselves, and position it to fit snugly into the spine of the white card. Working quickly and evenly from the spine outwards along all the edges, glue and fix the blue paper, making sure that the card will open and close successfully.

Using fine-bladed scissors, cut out the yacht template and prepare five white paper yachts. Cut out paper scraps to make boldly coloured hulls. Use a sharp pencil and straight edge to outline the mast and boom on each boat. Colour and add a different pennant to each, using pencils or inks.

Open the card and, using a tiny dot of glue or a narrow strip of double-sided tape on the back of each hull, secure one yacht to the short, vertical face of each pop-up bar, concealing as much of the bar as possible. It is easiest to work from the spine forwards, fixing yachts to the shorter bars first.

pop-out boxes

A small elastic band and a crochet hook create a simple but ingenious spring action. Inside a tight-fitting envelope, it is a surprise just waiting to happen.

Birthday Surprise
See page 66

Photocopy the template on page 117 on thin card. If joining papers, use a glue stick to avoid wrinkles. (Here shown as blue outside, ochre inside.) Lay the paper/card face down, draw round the template and cut out, taking special care with the acute angles. Turn the template over to mark and cut the reverse half.

Working on the outside surface of each half of the box and using the template as a guide, score very carefully with a craft knife and straight edge along all the dotted lines. Practise on a piece of joined paper or off-cut card to assess the correct pressure for the job. Accurate cutting and scoring are vital.

Fold each half inwards along the scored lines and reopen. Lay one half face down and, doubling the ribbon to form a decorative loop for hanging, tape the loose ends at the edge of the central hexagon so that the loop faces outwards and can be pulled through to the outside as the box is assembled.

For the Birthday Surprise you will need:

Template on page 117 • Thin card • Two complementary thick papers or double-sided thin card • Glue stick (for paper) • Pencil • Craft knife • Cutting mat • Straight edge • Ribbon • Adhesive tape • All-purpose glue • Stick-on shapes and sequins • Rubber band • Crochet hook

Expanding Football
See page 74

Before glueing the two halves together, check which of the two possible alignments is the more accurate and mark discreetly. Carefully squeeze a thin line of glue along all the flaps of one piece, including those with the hooks. Take care not to over-glue as this could cause a flap to stick to the inside of the box.

Keeping the ribbon to the outside and away from the glue, join the two halves, matching each edge exactly. Weight the box until dry. Decorate the facets with stick-ons and glued sequins, linking the design from face to face and leaving the top free for a message. (You may prefer to do this once the box is sprung.)

Hold the box slightly open with one hand and gently manoeuvre the rubber band inside the box and then over one of the paper hooks. Use the crochet hook to stretch the other end of the band across to the second hook. The card now has a spring action, folding flat only when it is squeezed.

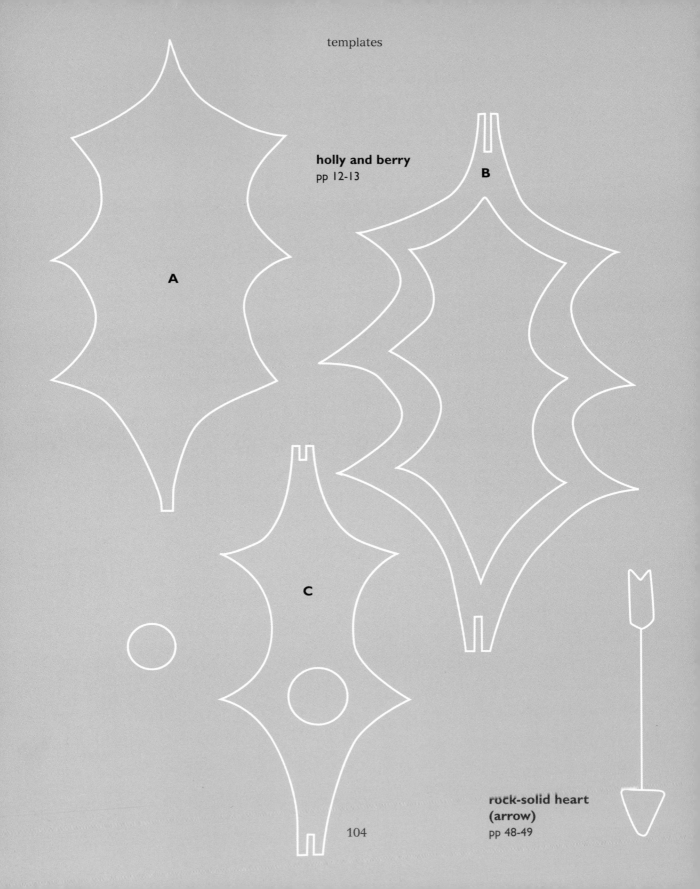

holly and berry
pp 12-13

A

B

C

104

**rock-solid heart
(arrow)**
pp 48-49

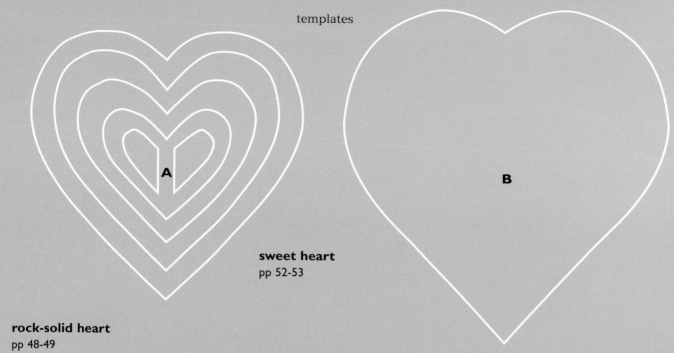

sweet heart
pp 52-53

rock-solid heart
pp 48-49

templates

golden bell
pp 14-15

snow crystal
pp 18-19

evergreen ring
pp 20-21

106

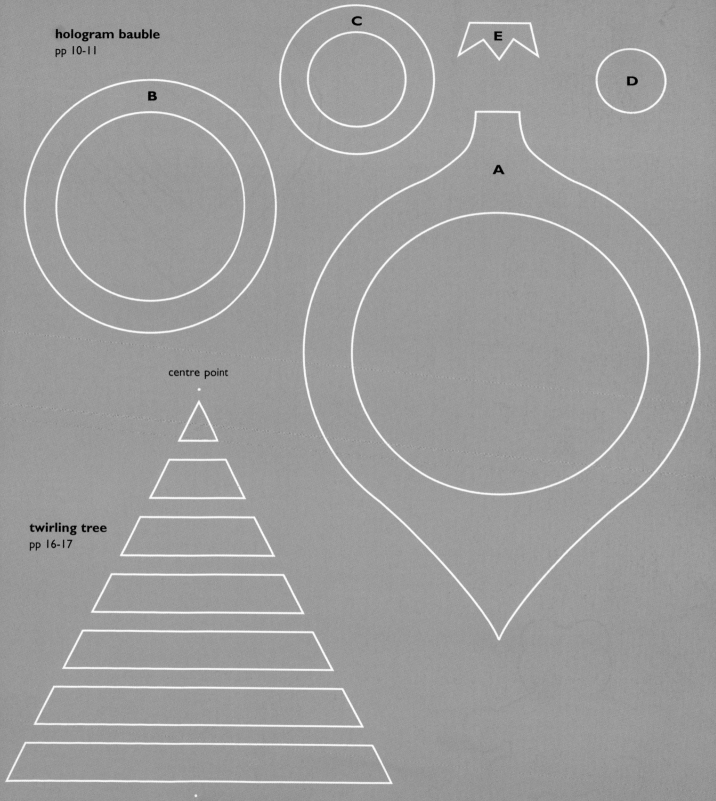

hologram bauble
pp 10-11

B

C

E

D

A

centre point

twirling tree
pp 16-17

centre point

star of david
pp 28-29

spinning teddy
pp 70-71

love birds
pp 56-57

moon and stars
pp 30-31

easter egg
pp 32-33

silver fish
pp 34-35

farewell wishes
pp 38-39

lucky horseshoe
pp 40-41

new home
pp 44-45

candle glow
pp 26–27

wedding bell
pp 58-59

A

wedding bell
pp 58-59

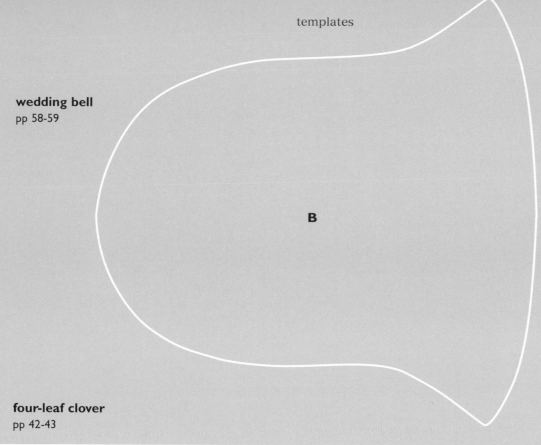

B

four-leaf clover
pp 42-43

blue marina
pp 64-65

dancing snowmen
pp 22-23

birthday surprise
pp 66-67

centre point

soft hearted
pp 50-51

centre point

rustic sunflower
pp 68-69

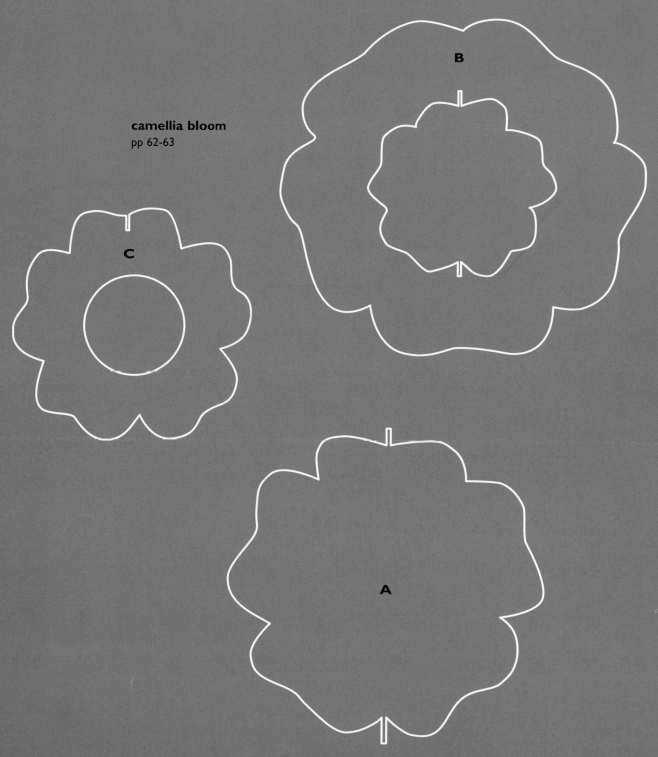

camellia bloom
pp 62-63

C

B

A

slotted cogs
pp 72-73

A

B

C

champagne celebration
pp 54-55

120

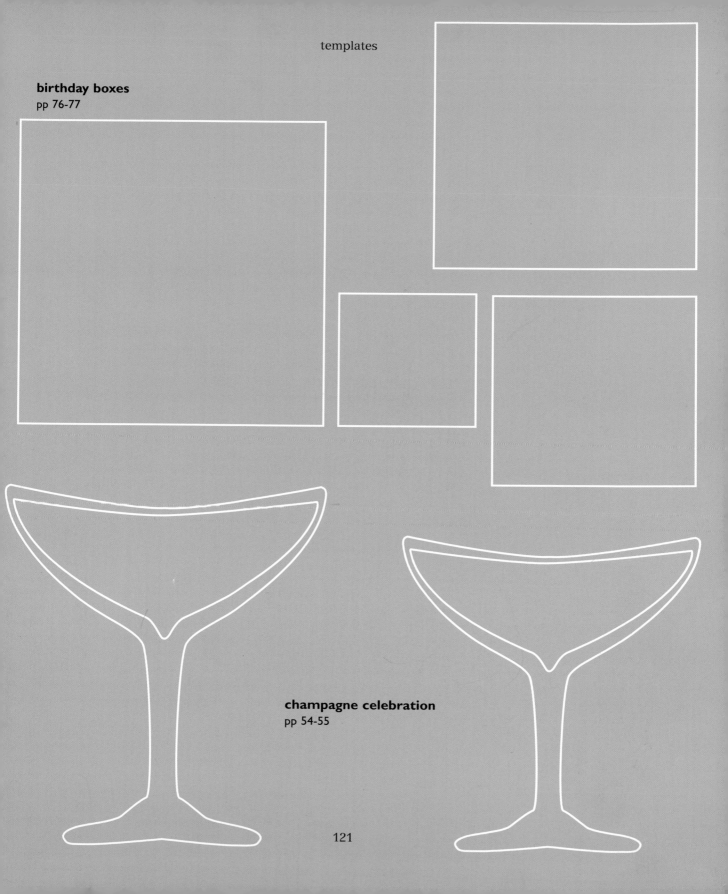

templates

birthday boxes
pp 76-77

champagne celebration
pp 54-55

121

envelopes

A well-matched envelope adds a real polish to your hand-made card, but bear post-office guidance in mind if you are sending your greeting.

Choose the best proportioned template for your card from the selection on pages 123–125, and photocopy, enlarging by 200% so that your card will fit easily on the central rectangle or square. Cut out the template, transfer onto a piece of paper that matches your card, and cut out your envelope.

Using the dotted lines on the template as a guide, fold along the sides of the central rectangle, or square to form the flaps of your envelope. Open out the top and bottom flaps again, for gluing in step 3. If you wish to add a decorative border to the front of the envelope, do so at this stage before you glue the flaps.

Glue the lower edges of the two side flaps sparingly, taking great care that the glue does not ooze onto the reverse of the front of the envelope. Fold in the bottom snub-nosed flap onto the glued edges. Allow to dry before inserting the card. Finally seal with more glue, sticky tape, or decorative paper sticker.

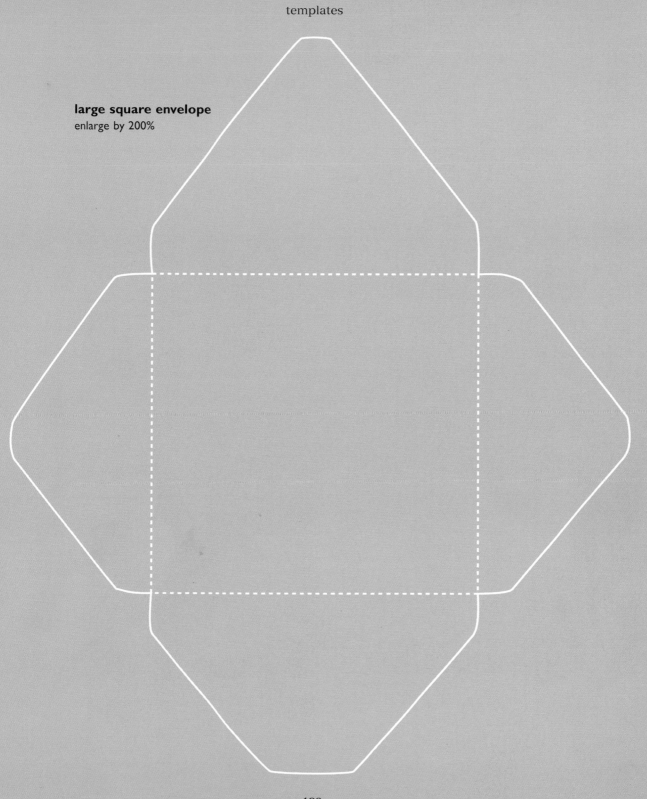

large square envelope
enlarge by 200%

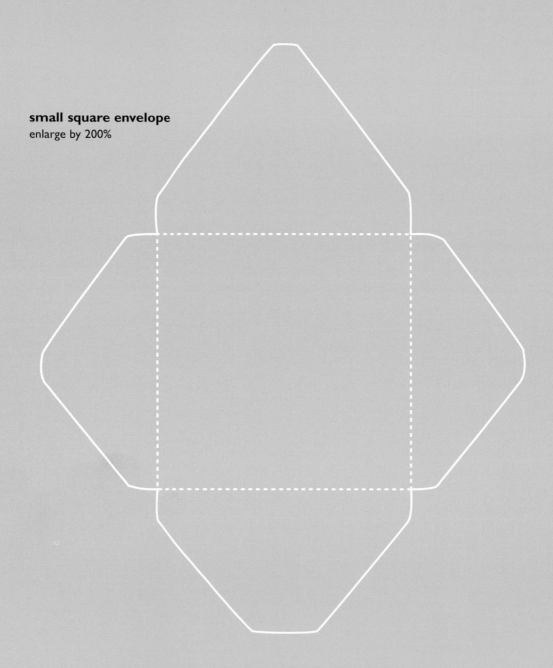

small square envelope
enlarge by 200%

small oblong envelope
enlarge by 200%

large oblong envelope
enlarge by 200%

index